The Jesus Bible

STUDY SERIES

BEGINNINGS

THE STORY OF HOW ALL THINGS WERE CREATED BY GOD AND FOR GOD

Aaron Coe
Series Writer & General Editor of *The Jesus Bible*

Matt Rogers
Series Writer & Lead Writer of *The Jesus Bible*

Beginnings Bible Study Guide

Requests for information should be addressed to:
HarperChristian Resources, 3900 Sparks Dr. SE, Grand Rapids, Michigan 49546

ISBN 978-0-310-15498-3 (softcover)
ISBN 978-0-310-15499-0 (ebook)

HarperChristian Resources titles may be purchased in bulk for church, business, fundraising, or ministry use. For information, please e-mail ResourceSpecialist@ChurchSource.com.

First printing December 2022 / Printed in the United States of America

CONTENTS

INTRODUCTION

You have a story.

Everyone does.

And while your story is unique, all of our stories are alike in some ways.

Every story has a beginning. We were born on a specific date and in a particular place in the world. From that time, we began to grow and emerge into the people we are today.

We also all have an end. There will be a date in the future—one that we do not yet know—when our time on this earth will be finished. These dates of our birth and death serve as the first and last pages of the story of our lives.

Yet that is likely where our similarities end. Our births were not all the same. Some of us were given to two parents who marked our birth with a steady stream of pictures, praise, and parties. Others among us never knew our parents and emerged into the world with little fanfare. We spent time in cities that ranged from cosmopolitan hubs to rural mill villages. Our education and development were markedly altered as a result of the place we called home.

While common themes are found in everyone's story, no two people experience the same set of joyful circumstances or painful events. The start of a relationship, birth of a child, and reunion with an old friend are only a few of the joyful factors that inform the chapters of our lives—while divorce, tragedy, and addiction represent just a few of the painful factors that will also inform our lives. And though we will all die, the details of our death will differ as well. Some of us will live to a ripe old age and pass from this life surrounded by our closest family and friends, while others of us will face an untimely death. Sadly, some of us may even leave a legacy of pain and destruction in our wake.

You live *your* story. Yet it's likely that on most days, you have found it hard to figure out exactly where your story is going. You might be thinking that your life is a little off. You might be wondering, "What is the purpose in it all?" You might be questioning some of the pain you have experienced, or some of the poor choices that you've made, or battling a nagging sense of anxiety about what is coming in the days ahead.

The reality is that you cannot understand the meaning of your life apart from Jesus. The *only* way to understand your story is by connecting it to a larger story.

God's story isn't like the one that you have. For one thing, you can already know the beginning and ending of God's story and all the major details in between. You can know who God is, what he is like, and what he is doing in the world. You can know why he created all things—including *you*—and how he is going to save sinners and fix a broken world.

God's story also differs from your own because it never changes. You don't have to worry that some unforeseen event is going to divert God's plan or change his mind. God, because he is gracious, reveals his unchanging story to you through the Bible.

It might be helpful to think of the story of Scripture as being told through six main acts: (1) **Beginnings**, (2) **Revolt**, (3) **People**, (4) **Savior**, (5) **Church**, (6) **Forever**. Every detail in the Bible can be placed into one of these six acts. They tell God's story from beginning to end.

This study, *Beginnings*, is designed to usher you through the first act of God's story, which is revealed most fully in the opening two chapters of the book of Genesis. Later biblical authors also wrote about God's creation and the purposes behind his work, so we will pull from those portions of Scripture as well as we go along.

Throughout *Beginnings*, you will discover that your story begins with a creating God. The text of the Bible underscores that *you* are created in his image. Your origination was thus in the mind of a majestic God. Everything beautiful, spiritual, wonderful, and eternal about you is the result of his divine image woven into your spirit from the start.

You will also see how the triune God worked through the Son to bring about the creation of everything. "For in [Jesus] all things were created: things in heaven and on earth, visible and invisible, whether thrones or powers or rulers or authorities; all things have been created through him and for him" (Colossians 1:16). In the beginning, Jesus created everything.

Our prayer is that *Beginnings* will be far more than just another Bible study. It is our hope that as you start to grasp God's greater story, you will begin to make greater sense of the story of your life. It is also our goal that you will come to understand the amazing truth that *God has actually included you in his story*! From the dawn of creation, he was thinking of you and designed your life to play a key role in the outworking of the story he's writing.

His story is best understood from the beginning. So that's where we'll start.

In the beginning . . .

— AARON & MATT

Lesson 1

CREATION

In the beginning God created the heavens and the earth.

GENESIS 1:1

For in [Jesus] all things were created: things in heaven and on earth, visible and invisible.

COLOSSIANS 1:16

By the word
of the LORD
the heavens
were made ...

— PSALM 33:6

WELCOME

Many books, movies, poems, and speeches are famous for their opening lines. I'm guessing that when I say the phrase, "A long time ago in a galaxy far, far away . . ." you immediately think of *Star Wars*. Or when I say the line, "Four score and seven years ago our fathers brought forth on this continent a new nation . . ." you recognize it as President Lincoln's opening line to the Gettysburg Address, one of the most important speeches in American history.

Opening lines set the context. They help the audience know where the story is going. Additionally, and perhaps more importantly, opening lines of a story help the reader understand the magnitude of what is about to be discussed.

For instance, when Abraham Lincoln delivered the Gettysburg Address, he knew he would have to grab his listeners' attention quickly. His speech was to follow several hours of dialogue from other speakers on that day—including a two-hour oration about the Battle of Gettysburg and its significance. Lincoln understood that if his audience was going to grasp the gravity of the situation, they would do so in the first few words that he spoke.

In the same way, the God of the universe—who exists in eternity and has no beginning or ending—entered into the space and time of human history with these attention-grabbing words: "In the beginning God created the heavens and the earth" (Genesis 1:1). These opening words of Scripture convey the scene at the dawn of creation where we first encounter an eternal God hovering over a formless expanse. There was nothing—except God.

Into the void, God spoke. His words thundered with power. "And God said, 'Let there be light,' and there was light" (verse 3). His words were not like the frail and insignificant words that we humans often use. They were mighty and strong—powerful enough to bring beauty from chaos and light from darkness. At the sound of his voice, creation burst to life.

1. When was the last time you were overwhelmed by the beauty, power, or majesty of something? What was it? How did it make you feel and how did you respond?

READ

God's Power in Creation

The disciple John would later point to the magnitude of God's creative work when he wrote in his Gospel, "Through him all things were made; without him nothing was made that has been made" (John 1:3). *All things*. God made *everything*. There's nothing in all the universe that was not intricately crafted by him. God often reminded his people throughout the Scriptures of the majesty of his creation. We see this in the story of Job, an Old Testament saint who suffered mightily. As the following passage relates, he was given a picture of God's power at creation, and God reminded him that there was much more to his story than he alone could grasp.

[1] *Then the Lord spoke to Job out of the storm. He said:*

[2] *"Who is this that obscures my plans*
with words without knowledge?
[3] *Brace yourself like a man;*
I will question you,
and you shall answer me.

[4] *"Where were you when I laid the earth's foundation?*
Tell me, if you understand.
[5] *Who marked off its dimensions? Surely you know!*
Who stretched a measuring line across it?
[6] *On what were its footings set,*
or who laid its cornerstone—
[7] *while the morning stars sang together*
and all the angels shouted for joy?

[8] *"Who shut up the sea behind doors*
when it burst forth from the womb,
[9] *when I made the clouds its garment*
and wrapped it in thick darkness,
[10] *when I fixed limits for it*
and set its doors and bars in place,
[11] *when I said, 'This far you may come and no farther;*
here is where your proud waves halt'?

[12] *"Have you ever given orders to the morning,*
or shown the dawn its place,
[13] *that it might take the earth by the edges*
and shake the wicked out of it?
[14] *The earth takes shape like clay under a seal;*
its features stand out like those of a garment.
[15] *The wicked are denied their light,*
and their upraised arm is broken.

[16] *"Have you journeyed to the springs of the sea*
or walked in the recesses of the deep?

[17] *Have the gates of death been shown to you?*
Have you seen the gates of the deepest darkness?
[18] *Have you comprehended the vast expanses of the earth?*
Tell me, if you know all this.

[19] *"What is the way to the abode of light?*
And where does darkness reside?

[20] *Can you take them to their places?*
Do you know the paths to their dwellings?

[21] *Surely you know, for you were already born!*
You have lived so many years!

Job 38:1–21

2. How does God describe his power to Job in these verses?

3. What does this passage reveal about the way God cares for his creation?

Maker of Heaven and Earth

The writers of Scripture continually described God as "the Maker of heaven and earth" (Psalm 146:6). The authors point to this truth more than 100 times in the Bible. The church made a similar claim in its earliest creeds. The Apostles' Creed begins with these words: "I believe in God the Father, Almighty Maker of heaven and earth." The early church understood that a foundational claim of the Christian faith rests on the fact that the God we worship made all that exists. His creation is grand because it's a reflection of his character. In fact, as the following passage relates, creation is meant to point back to the Creator and declare his excellence.

> [18] *The wrath of God is being revealed from heaven against all the godlessness and wickedness of people, who suppress the truth by their wickedness,* [19] *since what may be known about God is plain to them, because God has made it plain to them.* [20] *For since the creation of the world God's invisible qualities—his eternal power and divine nature—have been clearly seen, being understood from what has been made, so that people are without excuse.*
>
> [21] *For although they knew God, they neither glorified him as God nor gave thanks to him, but their thinking became futile and their foolish hearts were darkened.* [22] *Although they claimed to be wise, they became fools* [23] *and exchanged the glory of the immortal God for images made to look like a mortal human being and birds and animals and reptiles.*

[24] *Therefore God gave them over in the sinful desires of their hearts to sexual impurity for the degrading of their bodies with one another.* [25] *They exchanged the truth about God for a lie, and worshiped and served created things rather than the Creator—who is forever praised.*

Romans 1:18–25

4. What does Paul say we should be able to learn about God from his creation?

5. Why do you think it is so important for the church to continually remember that God is the Creator? Why does this matter for the Christian faith?

REFLECT

Focus on the Creator

"Every good and perfect gift is from above, coming down from the Father of the heavenly lights" (James 1:17). Unfortunately, much like kids on Christmas morning who look past their parents' generosity to the gifts themselves, we are prone to look right past the most significant aspect of creation and become enamored by the goodness of created things.

Certainly, there is much to love about the world God made. But what's truly spectacular about creation isn't actually creation at all—not the vast oceans, sprawling mountain ranges, or stunning sunsets. Those same oceans can erupt in tumultuous storms. Those mountains can crumble. That sun can be shrouded in clouds. What should inspire awe and wonder is the One who made it all—not only the *creation* itself, but also the *Creator.*

This very exchange—creation for Creator—lies at the core of all human sin. As Paul wrote in Romans 1, sinful people worship and serve the creature rather than the Creator. They discount or deny the Maker of heaven and earth and worship his handiwork—whether it's money, relationships, work, art, power, sports, science, or any other created thing. Every sin we've ever committed results from this exchange.

Think about how this plays out in business. People take the creativity they've been given by God and the beauty of the world he's made and use it to build lives that revolve around financial gain, creating structures that celebrate rebellion from God. Some do the same with their families. A spouse and children are great gifts—a clear demonstration of God's love and kindness. But no person, not even a family member, is meant to take God's place in our lives. If we choose to revolve our lives around our families, selfishly pursuing our private happiness and measuring the quality of our lives based on our families' wellbeing, we turn God's gifts into cheap substitutes for the gift-provider himself.

If it is true that all human failure and brokenness results from loving the creation more than the Creator, then *the most important thing we can do is remind ourselves of who this Creator is and what he is like.* This is a far better starting point than where we typically start. When we realize we've blown it and decide it's time to get our act together, we're prone to rely on our efforts and self-justification to try and earn our way back to God by our own merit.

We aren't going to start *Beginnings* with our view of our mistakes, regrets, and works. Rather, *we are going to begin with our view of God.* Our sins and failures result from a weak view of our Creator and a misguided love for the things he has made. So, we are going to begin with God—his greatness and his power. The more we glimpse the greatness of God, the more he transforms our lives into all he intended for us to be.

6. How are you tempted to love creation more than the Creator?

7. How are you using the gifts and talents God has provided to you for his glory, rather than only for earthly means?

Consider the Creator

The psalmist wrote, "May the glory of the Lord endure forever; may the Lord rejoice in his works—he who looks at the earth, and it trembles, who touches the mountains, and they smoke" (Psalm 104:31–32). Our world doesn't talk a lot about glory (at least, not rightly), but it's a concept we intuitively understand. Glory should capture our attention, cause us to gasp in awe, and overwhelm us with beauty or intricacy.

There's no real earthly comparison for God's glory. Even the first glimpse of a bride on her wedding day, the feeling you get when you stand on the rim of the Grand Canyon, or the view of the sun dipping below the horizon are nothing compared to the glory of God. Everything God made—all rolled into one big package—testifies to the glory of who he is. That's the point of creation—to inspire awe at the glory of the Creator.

You've probably had an experience like this at some point in your life. Maybe you were staring up at a star-filled sky or walking the shore of the beach. Deep inside, you were gripped by a sense of something bigger, more profound, and more powerful than you could see with your eyes. This "something" wasn't actually a *thing* but a *person*.

It was God.

Not only is it amazing to consider *that* God made everything, but it's also stunning to think about *how* he created it. God did not create like we do. People take existing material—things like instruments or wood—and use them to shape something else. We call it a new creation but, in reality, we've merely taken the existing creation and repackaged it.

God did something altogether different. He took nothing and made something. Scholars often refer to this as *ex nihilo*. You don't have to know Latin to guess at the meaning of that phrase—he made "out of nothing." The author of the book of Hebrews captures it this way: "What is seen was not made out of what was visible" (Hebrews 11:3). Talk about glory! Anyone who can make something out of nothing is glorious.

This answer to the "how" question continues to perplex many who read Scripture and are prone to want more details about exactly how God created. Using modern science as a guide, some want the Bible to read like a textbook, outlining the intricate details of the process God used to create all that is. There may be a time and place for such inquiry, but this is certainly not primary in the minds of the authors of Scripture. Instead, *God intended us to know that he created out of nothing in order to show his glory*. That's it.

8. What aspects of creation make you think there is, or might be, a Creator?

9. What can you learn about the Creator from what he has made?

CLOSE

God's creation is quite impressive (and that's an understatement!). The world is *beautiful*—from intricately designed flowers to countless majestic galaxies we are still discovering. God made the world extravagant and *orderly*—built to run in a certain way, making it possible for humans to mine the depths of God's wisdom through science. Creation is *complex*—astounding the greatest minds throughout human history.

Every aspect of creation reveals the sheer majesty of the glory of God. A glorious God made a good world. Long before sin distorted the earth, it was filled with peace, harmony, joy, beauty, and all other realities that we wish were true of the world in which we live. The broken world we experience is a far cry from Eden. The created world is broken—not because of an inherent fault in the Creator's design, but because of human failure and sin.

But human sin is no match for the power of the Creator! He is intent on his glory being seen, known, and worshiped. Sin is no match for someone powerful enough to speak all things into existence. And it's this God—the Maker of the heavens and earth—who is pursuing *you* with his love. He has promised that a day is coming when "the earth will be filled with the knowledge of the glory of the LORD as the waters cover the sea" (Habakkuk 2:14).

The waters cover the sea completely—there's no part of the sea not covered by water. Such will be true of our world. Currently, the glory of God is on display in his created world, though many fail to recognize him as the Creator. One day, there will be no mistaking his glory. It will be clearly seen and known throughout his world. We live in a time when sin and brokenness seem to prevail—but this is the time before God's glory will be seen by everyone.

It's vital that we rightly understand who God is and what He is doing in the world in the space between what is and what will one day be. We'll talk about that more in our next session.

10. Does God's involvement in the details of creation give you confidence in his involvement in the details of your life? How?

11. Just as all of creation is a reflection of God's glory, how can you be a reflection of his greatness this week?

Lesson 2

THE TRINITY

"Let us make mankind in our image, after our likeness."

GENESIS 1:26

"Therefore go and make disciples of all nations, baptizing them in the name of the Father and of the Son and of the Holy Spirit."

MATTHEW 28:19

The love of God ...

... the fellowship of

the Holy Spirit ...

... be with you all.

— 2 CORINTHIANS 13:14

WELCOME

I grew up in Kentucky. As you may know, the sport of basketball is huge in the state. I like to say that in Kentucky we use football to get in shape for basketball season . . . which usually frustrates all the diehard football fans out there!

In basketball, each team has five players on the floor at one time. Each person is given a specific position and role. However, unlike football or baseball, the roles and the positions are fluid. No player on a basketball court stays in the same spot. Each player has to adjust to what the situation calls for and help out the other players on the team. This is the only way the team can achieve its overall goal of winning basketball games.

Regardless of how independent or self-sufficient we perceive ourselves, the simple fact is we cannot do life on our own. Our survival would be impossible without help. Fortunately, God, in his infinite grace, desires to have a relationship with humanity. He is not a far-off deity who is disengaged from our affairs. No, he wants to be involved. He wants relationship.

In the Trinity, we see God's *model* and *plan* for his relationship with us. As a model, the Trinity shows how interaction between distinct persons can be achieved. And as a plan, we see how each person of the Trinity carries a distinct role, yet are unified together in a mission.

From the beginning, we see that God manifests himself in three persons: Father, Son, and Holy Spirit. Each person of the Trinity, while being fully God, represents itself in three distinct ways.

God the Father serves as the ultimate authority. He is the creator and the author, and from him everything has its genesis.

God the Son serves as the physical presence of God. He took on flesh and dwelled among us on earth so that he could identify with humanity and ultimately serve as the sacrifice for our salvation.

God the Holy Spirit serves as our power source. The book of Acts tells us that humanity will receive its "power" when the Holy Spirit comes. Everything we need for life is found supremely in the Trinity.

The idea of God in multiple persons is found in the creation narrative. From the beginning, we see God not in the *singular* but in the *plural* form. Genesis 1:26 says, "Let us make mankind in our image, in our likeness." This indication, from the beginning, is backed up all throughout Scripture as a reference to the three distinct persons, or manifestations, of God.

1. Have you ever worked on something so big you could not do it by yourself? What was it? Who was there to guide or help you?

2. How would you describe the relationship that you currently have with God?

READ

The Authority of the Father

From the beginning, God has been on a mission, and the ultimate mission of God is his glory. The purpose of humanity is to find our ultimate satisfaction and enjoyment in God by bringing glory to him.

When we are under God's authority, there is great freedom in knowing that we don't have to make life up as we go. We have been empowered by someone else to execute the right mission.

On the surface, this may fly in the face of our sensibilities. We love our freedom and autonomy. However, when we realize that God has set up boundaries for our good, we recognize that great security and flourishing life are found within those bounds.

God the Father is not only on a mission, but he has also sent his people on a mission. One of the ways he fulfills his mission to glorify himself is by redeeming humanity for his glory. As one New Testament theologian noted, "Mission proceeds from an authority that sends envoys and a message to other people and to other places."[1] The apostle Paul writes:

> [4] *But when the set time had fully come, God sent his Son, born of a woman, born under the law,* [5] *to redeem those under the law, that we might receive adoption to sonship.*
>
> Galatians 4:4–5

> [15] *But when God, who set me apart from my mother's womb and called me by his grace, was pleased* [16] *to reveal his Son in me so that I might preach him among the Gentiles, my immediate response was not to consult any human being.*
>
> Galatians 1:15–16

Just like God sent Jesus and Paul on mission, he is sending us today. We can operate in freedom, knowing that he doesn't leave us to ourselves to make up a mission and accomplish it in our own strength. He has a plan for us that was set in motion before we were born.

3. What do these passages in Galatians reveal about the role of God in "sending"?

4. In these passages, when did God set Jesus and Paul apart for their missions?

The Presence of the Son and Power of the Spirit

Not only does God send us into life with a plan, but he sends us with a person. In Jesus, we have a model for how human life should look. God the Son, in the person of Jesus, lived a fully human, yet fully divine, life on earth. In his divinity, he had the full character of God, as illustrated by his ability to raise the dead, walk on water, heal the sick, and perform many other miracles. In his humanity, he was Emmanuel—God with us. He was able to identify with human suffering, weakness, and temptation. As Paul writes:

> [5] *In your relationships with one another, have the same mindset as Christ Jesus:*
>
> [6] *Who, being in very nature God,*
> *did not consider equality with God something to be used*
> *to his own advantage;*
>
> [7] *rather, he made himself nothing*
> *by taking the very nature of a servant,*
> *being made in human likeness.*

[8] *And being found in appearance as a man,*
he humbled himself
by becoming obedient to death—
even death on a cross!

[9] *Therefore God exalted him to the highest place*
and gave him the name that is above every name,

[10] *that at the name of Jesus every knee should bow,*
in heaven and on earth and under the earth,

[11] *and every tongue acknowledge that Jesus Christ is Lord,*
to the glory of God the Father.

Philippians 2:5–11

There is more to learn from the life of Jesus than we could ever comprehend. One of those great lessons is that we are called to humble ourselves and serve others. Most of us will not be led to the point of death in our servanthood, but still our lives should be marked by willing self-sacrifice, and Jesus shows us the way.

If we are not careful, we could get overwhelmed and discouraged by considering an obedient Christian life to be impossible. We can (rightly) think that there is no way to follow Jesus' model to perfection. God knew we would need help in living this life and that we would battle sin to the end. Simply following a guide or a model in our own strength is not enough to live an obedient life. We need a helper and an encourager along the way.

The Holy Spirit is that helper, sent by God to help us live life to the fullest. In John 14:26, Jesus tells us, "The Helper, the Holy Spirit, whom the Father will send in My name, He will teach you all things" (NKJV).

Notice, once again, who the "sender" is. God sent the Holy Spirit to help us by reminding us of everything true and right. When we don't know the right decision to make or what the wise choice would be, the Holy Spirit is there to help us.

The Holy Spirit wants to keep us from making decisions that are not in God's plan for us. In the book of Acts, we read how the apostle Paul wanted to go to Asia to preach the gospel and made plans for travelling there. However, God had others plans:

> [6] *Paul and his companions traveled throughout the region of Phrygia and Galatia, having been kept by the Holy Spirit from preaching the word in the province of Asia.* [7] *When they came to the border of Mysia, they tried to enter Bithynia, but the Spirit of Jesus would not allow them to.* [8] *So they passed by Mysia and went down to Troas.* [9] *During the night Paul had a vision of a man of Macedonia standing and begging him, "Come over to Macedonia and help us."* [10] *After Paul had seen the vision, we got ready at once to leave for Macedonia, concluding that God had called us to preach the gospel to them.*
>
> Acts 16:6–10

On the surface, Paul's desire to go to Asia to preach the gospel seemed to be a noble thing. but it was not God's best. It was not what he had in mind for Paul and his team. Likewise, God wants what is best for us, and the Holy Spirit is there to guide us toward that best.

5. In Philippians 2:5–11, how does Jesus model how humans should live?

6. In the story told in Acts, why do you think the Holy Spirit prevented Paul and Barnabas from going to Asia and Bithynia? Where did the Holy Spirit eventually lead them?

REFLECT

Depicting God in Three Persons

If you were to try to pick an image to communicate what God is like, what would you choose? How would you portray the glory of God? How might you communicate the Trinity as one God existing eternally in three persons?

The question you just considered has challenged thinkers throughout history as they have tried to find ways to capture the relationship between the Father, the Son, and the Holy Spirit. It's common for people to use images like water, which can exist in three forms—ice, liquid, and steam—to describe the relationship. But water can't exist in each of these three forms at the same time, whereas God is always Father, Son, and Spirit.

Others have used human relationships or roles as a way to portray the three persons of God. A man, for example, can simultaneously exist as a husband, a father, and a son. But this idea, while helpful, also doesn't capture the essence of God, as it refers to the man's relationship to someone else and not his identity in himself.

A man is a husband because he is married, and he stops being a husband if his marriage ends. Yet God is always Father, Son, and Spirit. This isn't just the way God relates to people, and he will never stop existing in each of these persons. Simply put, there is no way to represent God fully and accurately with an earthly image.

If there is a God who is eternal, all-powerful, and all-wise, we should expect that it would be hard to talk about that God using human language and images. In fact, if God had not been gracious to reveal himself to people in the first place, we'd have no way of knowing all the details we do know about him now. The persons who make up God become clearer when we read the Bible and see how God has put himself on display.

Throughout history, it has become common to use a word, rather than an image, to refer to the three persons of God as the "Trinity." Surprising to some, this word is not found in the Bible, but as we've seen, the concept of a singular God who manifests himself in three persons is the picture that emerges as we read God's story. Each person—Father, Son, and Spirit—is equally God, yet has a differing role in God's plan to display his glory, save sinners, and restore a broken world.

If your brain hurts at this point, you are in good company. You might be new to thinking deeply about God, so expect it to feel a bit like returning to the gym for a workout after one-too-many late-night trips to get fast food. You're going to be sore. However, rather than taking this as a sign to give up, allow it to push you forward to grow in your knowledge of God and appreciation of his glory.

True, you will never understand everything about God. He's just too big for that. But you can know God. God himself promised that if you seek him with all your heart, you will find him (see Jeremiah 29:12). Even though the Trinity is a challenging concept, it's important to know God rightly so you can understand and respond properly to the God you seek to worship.

7. In what area of your life are you most and least likely to push yourself to grow and mature?

8. Are you more likely to strive to grow or excuse yourself out of genuine effort? Explain.

Growing in Knowledge and Worship of the Creator

The effort you pour into spiritual growth will always be worthwhile, because it is the one area of life that has eternal value. Paul wrote that while efforts like physical training are of some value, godliness, or spiritual training, is of value in every way because it holds promise for the present life and the life to come (see 1 Timothy 4:8).

You might seek to develop your physical body through regular exercise and healthy eating, but in the end, your body will wear out, and eventually you will die. But growing in knowledge and worship of God will last forever. As we saw in lesson 1, true change takes place when you grow in love and worship of your Creator.

Paul often ended his letters by entrusting the recipients to the care of the Father, Son, and Holy Spirit. For example, his lengthy second letter to the church at Corinth ends this way: "May the grace of the Lord Jesus Christ, and the love of God, and the fellowship of the Holy Spirit be with you all" (2 Corinthians 13:14). The Trinity brings grace, love, and fellowship.

We're not just talking about some abstract theological concept, but a proper understanding of the one true God who is capable of providing all you deeply need. Think about how many of your friends and family go through life clamoring for grace, love, and fellowship. All of these things can be found perfectly in the Father, Son, and Spirit.

9. How does your life demonstrate a need for grace, love, and fellowship?

10. How can the Trinity provide those qualities in ways that no one or nothing else on this earth can?

CLOSE

Much more could be said about each person of God, and we will continue discussing them in later lessons. For now, it is important to remember that God always has and always will exist in these three persons. They encompass the totality of who God is. They give shape and form to his name, which is one, and will never change. This is who God always was before any person was ever created, and this is who he will be long after our lives are over.

The fixed nature of God provides great hope to ever-changeable people like us. You have likely experienced the shiftiness of people—one day they feel and act a certain way, and the next they have changed completely. Worse still, you have probably seen this trend in your own life.

We are changeable people. But God is unchanging. We don't have to worry that we might get to know God and learn about his character and work in the world, only to find one day that he has totally changed. He is the great I AM who was, and is, and is to come. He is worthy of our trust as we spend our lives pressing on to know the God who never changes.

11. What has God taught you about the Trinity in this session?

12. In what ways will your deeper understanding of the Trinity impact your day-to-day life?

Note

1. Eckhard J. Schnabel, *Paul the Missionary: Realities, Strategies, and Methods* (Downers Grove, IL: IVP Academic, 2008), p. 23.

Lesson 3

IMAGO DEI

So God created mankind in his own image . . .

GENESIS 1:27

To them God has chosen to make known among the Gentiles the glorious riches of this mystery, which is Christ in you, the hope of glory.

COLOSSIANS 1:27

Put on the new self,
created to be
like God in true
righteousness . . .

— EPHESIANS 4:24

WELCOME

Every great artist has a defining work. Musicians or poets might have a *lifetime* of work, but there is often a single piece that serves to encompass their *best* work. The *Mona Lisa* is such a work in Leonardo da Vinci's masterful career, and it's tough to top Michelangelo's handiwork on the Sistine Chapel. The pinnacle of these artists' brilliance is seen in their defining work.

It's hard to imagine applying the same principle to God. As a Creator, he's made some pretty amazing things. Animals, plants, oceans, mountains, stars, and sky—and the universe itself. How would you go about organizing them into a top-ten list of God's all-time greats?

Thankfully, the Bible answers that question. You won't find a ranked list of various animals or plants that God made, but you will notice that one aspect of God's creation is elevated above all the others. The opening chapter of Genesis describes God's work in creation by summarizing what he made on each day, and there's a repetitious conclusion at the end of each day's work. God looked at all that he had made and saw that it was good.

The word *good* seems like a weak way to describe the creation of light, oceans, and elephants—until you remember this is the perfect God of the universe doing the creating. If he says something is good, you can rest assured that he knows what he's talking about!

But then we come to the last day of creation, when God makes the first human. God takes dust from the ground, fashions it into a person, and breathes life into this body.

However, unlike the rest of creation, we discover that "God created mankind in his own image" (Genesis 1:27). Humans are the *only* beings on this earth who were created *imago Dei*—in the very image and likeness of their Creator.

Importantly, the day that God makes humans finishes with a slightly different evaluation from the Lord. He doesn't just see that what he has created is *good*. Rather, he looks at this act of his creation and deems it "very good" (Genesis 1:31).

1. Thinking about your family heritage, what are some defining characteristics found in your family tree?

2. Have you ever stopped to think about the fact that God's characteristics are found in you? What impact should that have on how you view yourself?

READ

Human Beings Are God's Masterpiece

The climax of God's creation—his defining work—is a person. And this person is not just any human being—he is the head of the entire human race. Everyone who ever lives will descend from this man. He is also not ordinary because God gives him a unique identity:

[26] Then God said, "Let us make mankind in our image, in our likeness, so that they may rule over the fish in the sea and the birds in the sky, over the livestock and all the wild animals, and over all the creatures that move along the ground."

[27] So God created mankind in his own image,
in the image of God he created them;
male and female he created them.

Genesis 1:26–27

The easiest way to pick up on what the biblical authors think is important is to notice the ideas or words they repeat. Twice in this passage we read that mankind is created in God's image, and we also read that this man is created after God's likeness. This is what makes people different from anything else God created—we are made in the *imago Dei* (in the image of God).

Long after God created humans, it became common for kings to use their image or likeness, often in the form of a statue, to represent their presence and power throughout the regions they controlled. People were meant to look at the image and be reminded of the king. We find this type of image being used for this purpose in the following account:

[1] King Nebuchadnezzar made an image of gold, sixty cubits high and six cubits wide, and set it up on the plain of Dura in the province of Babylon. [2] He then summoned the satraps, prefects, governors, advisers, treasurers, judges, magistrates and all the other provincial officials to come to the dedication of the image he had set up. [3] So the satraps, prefects, governors, advisers, treasurers, judges, magistrates and all the other provincial officials assembled for the dedication of the image that King Nebuchadnezzar had set up, and they stood before it.

[4] Then the herald loudly proclaimed, "Nations and peoples of every language, this is what you are commanded to do: [5] As soon as you hear the sound of the horn, flute, zither, lyre, harp, pipe and all kinds of music, you must fall down and worship the image of gold that King Nebuchadnezzar has set up.

[6] Whoever does not fall down and worship will immediately be thrown into a blazing furnace."

[7] Therefore, as soon as they heard the sound of the horn, flute, zither, lyre, harp and all kinds of music, all the nations and peoples of every language fell down and worshiped the image of gold that King Nebuchadnezzar had set up.

Daniel 3:1–7

Daniel refused to bow down to the statue of the king because he understood that worship was meant for God alone. God did not choose to set up carved statues of himself throughout the world. Instead, he created people. In fact, the Bible is full of commands that forbid God's people from making replicas of his image like the other cultures did in creating pagan statues of their false gods (see Exodus 20:4–6).

We aren't supposed to make images of God. We are each meant to *be* images of God. While God's presence still permeates this world, he is not physically present with people in a tangible manner. So we are to reflect his character so all creation will be constantly reminded of the power and presence of God and recognize him as the rightful King.

Even if you've never read or heard God's story in the Bible, you know how this mission has played out. The world you live in, and the people you meet, more often than not do a poor job of reflecting the image of God. The cause of this failure is described in heinous detail in Genesis 3, and the implications of this failure are seen in the stories that follow.

After sin leads to the first murder and chaos reigns on the earth (see Genesis 4–6), God determines to judge the world with a massive flood. Only one righteous man, Noah, and his family are spared (see Genesis 7–8). After the waters of the flood recede, God speaks to Noah and the others who are saved from his wrath about the identity of humans. He says that they are not to kill one another because they are made "in the image of God" (Genesis 9:6). Sin affected God's creation in innumerable ways, but it did not destroy the image of God in humanity. This image is now twisted, distorted, and marred by sin, but it is not lost forever.

3. What evidence do you see of the image of God in other people?

4. What feelings, beliefs, or actions (of yourself or others) prove that God's image in us has been affected by sin?

Implications of Being Made in God's Image

The fact we were created in the image of God necessitates two conclusions about our lives. The first conclusion is that the lives we were meant to live can only be experienced in relationship to God. It is impossible to "image" God unless we have a relationship with him. Unlike animals, we have the unique capacity to know God, talk to him, and live in communion with the Trinity in an intimate way (see John 15:1–17).

In fact, the Bible tells us that people were made by God and for God (see Colossians 1:16). It's no wonder all people have some religious hunger or awareness. They might deny these cravings or sedate them with all sorts of pseudo-gods, but deep inside all people is a craving for the relationship with God they were meant to experience. In the book of Acts, we read how Paul pointed out this truth to a group of philosophers in Athens:

> [22] *Paul then stood up in the meeting of the Areopagus and said: "People of Athens! I see that in every way you are very religious.* [23] *For as I walked around and looked carefully at your objects of worship, I even found an altar with this inscription:* TO AN UNKNOWN GOD. *So you are ignorant of the very thing you worship—and this is what I am going to proclaim to you.*
>
> [24] *"The God who made the world and everything in it is the Lord of heaven and earth and does not live in temples built by human hands.* [25] *And he is not served by human hands, as if he needed anything. Rather, he himself gives everyone life and breath and everything else.* [26] *From one man he made all the nations, that they should inhabit the whole earth; and he marked out their appointed times in history and the boundaries of their lands.* [27] *God did this so that they would seek him and perhaps reach out for him and find him, though he is not far from any one of us.* [28] *'For in him we live and move and have our being.' As some of your own poets have said, 'We are his offspring.'*
>
> [29] *"Therefore since we are God's offspring, we should not think that the divine being is like gold or silver or stone—an image made by human design and skill.* [30] *In the past God overlooked such ignorance, but now he commands all people everywhere to repent.* [31] *For he has set a day when he will judge the world with justice by the man he has appointed. He has given proof of this to everyone by raising him from the dead."*
>
> Acts 17:22–31

The second conclusion we can reach is that we should give our lives to reflect God's image to a watching world. Much has been written in an attempt to define the exact nature of the *imago Dei* and what it means to be created in God's image. Some claim the *imago Dei* refers to certain physical or moral attributes that humans possess, while others believe the *imago Dei* is a moral compass that allows them to know, understand, and follow God's law.

Perhaps it's best to think about the *imago Dei* as a mission—a purpose for life. If men and women live in relationship with God, they are able to reflect his image. Image-bearing isn't just a description—it's also an assignment. For example, when a husband and wife serve one another in love, they illustrate to the world the way God acted in love to send Jesus to serve sinners (see Philippians 2:4–11). Or, when a college student follows God's calling on his or her life to choose a lower-salary career that serves the poor, that person shows the world that God cares for the marginalized and broken. Jesus told the following parable about this:

> [31] *"When the Son of Man comes in his glory, and all the angels with him, he will sit on his glorious throne.* [32] *All the nations will be gathered before him, and he will separate the people one from another as a shepherd separates the sheep from the goats.*
>
> [33] *He will put the sheep on his right and the goats on his left.*
>
> [34] *"Then the King will say to those on his right, 'Come, you who are blessed by my Father; take your inheritance, the kingdom prepared for you since the creation of the world.* [35] *For I was hungry and you gave me something to eat, I was thirsty and you gave me something to drink, I was a stranger and you invited me in,* [36] *I needed clothes and you clothed me, I was sick and you looked after me, I was in prison and you came to visit me.'*
>
> [37] *"Then the righteous will answer him, 'Lord, when did we see you hungry and feed you, or thirsty and give you something to drink?* [38] *When did we see you a stranger and invite you in, or needing clothes and clothe you?* [39] *When did we see you sick or in prison and go to visit you?'*

> [40] *"The King will reply, 'Truly I tell you, whatever you did for one of the least of these brothers and sisters of mine, you did for me.'*
>
> Matthew 25:31–40

5. What does it look like for people to seek God or "feel" their way toward him?

6. The mission to reflect God's image can be lived out in countless ways each day. What do you hope people perceive about God from his image reflected in your life?

REFLECT

Our Mission to the World

Adam and Eve, the first image-bearers, were meant to live in relationship with God and reflect his image to the world. They had unique access to God, which should have made it far easier to live in an intimate relationship with him. Before sin entered the world, they walked and talked with God freely in the Garden of Eden. They also had specific commands from God as to how they could reflect his image. They were to enjoy the bountiful goodness of God and work in meaningful ways to steward the world in which God placed them.

There was only one thing forbidden—they were not to eat of the tree of the knowledge of good and evil (Genesis 2:15–17). That's it! One action was off limits, and everything else was free for them to enjoy and enhance.

God's plan extended beyond Adam and Eve. God told them to "be fruitful and increase in number; fill the earth" (1:28). Had Adam and Eve been faithful to their relationship with God and to reflecting his image, they would have been able to multiply other image-bearers who would live to reflect his image as well. This process of fruitful multiplication, carried out over the centuries, could have resulted in an entire world being filled with reflections of God's image. The entire earth would have been filled with the glory of God.

Though that didn't happen, this same mission defines all those whom God creates, even today. We are all meant to live in an intimate relationship with our Creator and give our lives to reflect that image everywhere we go. The middle-aged businessman is meant to love God deeply and give his entrepreneurial gifts and financial resources in a way that shows the world what God is like. High school seniors are meant to make college decisions based on what will position them to serve God and others most fully. All of life's decisions are meant to be made through the perspective of our relationship with God and our mission to reflect that image.

7. What was Adam and Eve's mission? Likewise, what is your mission in this world?

8. What choices are you facing right now? How are you filtering those decisions through the lens of your relationship with God and your mission to reflect his image?

God's Plan to Rescue His Image-Bearers

Adam and Eve's relationship with God, and their mission from him, became exponentially more difficult once sin entered the world. Sin compromises our relationship with God because it is impossible for a sinful person—one not yet rescued and reconciled to God by the grace of Jesus—to have an intimate relationship with a holy God.

Furthermore, sin sabotages our mission. We now fill the earth with broken reflections of God's image rather than wholly accurate reflections. We would be doomed to fail at our life's purpose had God not done something to save his image-bearers.

His answer is not one you might imagine. He knew it was impossible for broken image-bearers to fix themselves. The damage done by sin was too vast—too extensive—for people to rebuild a relationship and re-engage in a mission on their own. So God didn't merely chastise them for their failure or shout at them to do better in their own strength. As Paul explains:

> [1] *As for you, you were dead in your transgressions and sins,* [2] *in which you used to live when you followed the ways of this world and of the ruler of the kingdom of the air, the spirit who is now at work in those who are disobedient.* [3] *All of us also lived among them at one time, gratifying the cravings of our flesh*

and following its desires and thoughts. Like the rest, we were by nature deserving of wrath. [4] *But because of his great love for us, God, who is rich in mercy,* [5] *made us alive with Christ even when we were dead in transgressions—it is by grace you have been saved.* [6] *And God raised us up with Christ and seated us with him in the heavenly realms in Christ Jesus,* [7] *in order that in the coming ages he might show the incomparable riches of his grace, expressed in his kindness to us in Christ Jesus.* [8] *For it is by grace you have been saved, through faith—and this is not from yourselves, it is the gift of God—* [9] *not by works, so that no one can boast.* [10] *For we are God's handiwork, created in Christ Jesus to do good works, which God prepared in advance for us to do.*

Ephesians 2:1-10

God chose to demonstrate his love for those he made by sending Jesus into the world. The writer of Hebrews says that Jesus was "the radiance of God's glory and the exact representation of his being" (Hebrews 1:3). Since Jesus is God, he is the perfect image-bearer. He was able to live in perfect intimacy with the Father and Spirit through his life, modeling the type of relationship that people were meant to have with the Trinity (see John 17).

Jesus also lived out his mission to reflect the image of God to the world perfectly. He was without sin. Never once did he act in a way that diminished or obscured the glory of God (see 1 Peter 2:22). He perfectly fulfilled the task of image-bearing given to Adam in the Garden.

But if this were all that Jesus did, broken image-bearers would still have a problem. We could look to Jesus and see an example of how our lives were meant to be lived, but we would be unable to follow that example because we would still be trapped in our sin.

This is why Paul's claim in 2 Corinthians 5:21 is one of the most astounding, jaw-dropping truths in human history: "God [the Father] made him who had no sin [Jesus] to be sin for us, so that in him we might become the righteousness of God." Jesus, the perfect image-bearer, did not simply live a perfect life and challenge us to follow his example. Rather, he lived a perfect life and then willingly gave that life to pay the price that our sin deserves. He died in our place to rescue us from sin so that we might have eternal life.

As if that's not enough, he also gave us the gift of perfect standing with God that he earned by living a sinless life. As broken image-bearers, all we have to do to have a relationship with God and live out the mission for which we were created is confess Jesus as Lord, believe in his resurrection, repent of our sin, and receive this gift by faith (see Romans 10:9; Ephesians 2:8–9).

9. What did Jesus do on your behalf to rescue you from sin?

10. What does it mean to have faith in Jesus?

CLOSE

The act of putting our faith in Christ initiates a life spent doing what we were created to do in the first place. We grow to know and love God and seek to reflect him to the world. But we don't undertake this work in our own power. We now have God living in us by his Spirit, empowering us to fulfill our image-bearing mission (see Romans 8:28–30).

The Spirit will bring progressive transformation to our lives so that we increasingly reflect God's image as we were made to do. Of course, we will not reflect him perfectly right away—and never completely this side of heaven. There will still be failures. We will still battle with the sin that easily entangles our lives (see Hebrews 12:1–2). But those who live by faith in Jesus will experience the transforming power of God remaking them in his image. One day, when Jesus returns and fixes this broken world, we will reflect him perfectly forever (see 1 John 3:1–2).

11. In what ways has God used this lesson to clarify your mission on earth?

12. What are some specific areas in your life where you need to wait on the Spirit's power?

Lesson 4

UNIQUENESS

. . . in the image of God he created them; male and female he created them.

GENESIS 1:27

But you are a chosen people, a royal priesthood, a holy nation, God's special possession.

1 PETER 2:9

Your works are
wonderful,
I know that
full well.

— PSALM 139:14

WELCOME

I previously mentioned that I grew up in the state of Kentucky and referenced how big of a deal basketball is there. Well, my wife's grandmother was a raving fan of University of Kentucky basketball. Anyone who knew her understood not to get in her way on game day.

One of her habits, when she watched her beloved Wildcats, was to record the games on her VCR. (If you were born after the year 2000, Google it). While she would watch the game live, she would yell and scream at an almost unbearable pitch. Ironically, when she would go back and watch the recording of the game, she would yell even louder and more confidently. Her enthusiasm was elevated, not diminished, by knowing how the game would turn out.

It is a rare gift in life to be able to see how a story turns out. Most of the time, we are living the ending in real time. However, when we look at Scripture, we get a picture of how things turn out. When we turn to the book of Revelation, we see how the story of the world ends. We get a glimpse of God's vision for the new heavens and the new earth. We learn that a new city, a new Jerusalem, will descend out of the sky. The old will pass away and the new will be established forever (see Revelation 21–22).

We also get a picture in the book of Revelation of the diversity in which God created mankind. We discover there will be multitudes of tribes and nations gathered around God's throne in the end. John, the book's author, says of this diversity: "I looked, and there before me was a great multitude that no one could count, from every nation, tribe, people and language, standing before the throne and before the Lamb" (7:9).

Every nation, tribe, people, and language! Imagine that. For most of us, this kind of diversity is unfathomable. Most of us, unless we lived in a major city, grew up around people who looked like us and talked like us.

This reality is not unique to one ethnic group. Most of the world's population grow up in communities where the people in their immediate vicinity reflect their own racial identity. However, regardless of what our current community looks like, if we are in Christ, our eternity will be spent surrounded by great diversity. It will be a rich symphony around the throne of God, worshiping him with one voice.

1. Have you ever thought about how the diversity of eternity should impact the way you live right now?

2. What does the multicultural environment of Revelation 7:9 say about our own uniqueness?

READ

Humanity: A Diverse Symphony Tuned for God's Glory

When you visit a major metropolitan city like New York, it's nearly impossible to ignore the diverse and eclectic nature of the place. You'll likely be surrounded by all kinds of different people, languages, music, art, and food you've never experienced before.

Uniqueness is part of God's intention for his world. We might have expected that when God set forth to fill the earth with reflections of his glory, he did so by creating identical image-bearers who all looked and acted exactly the same. It would be far easier to envision a world where people were united in this mission if everyone thought, talked, and behaved alike.

Even so, it's hard to imagine an infinitely creative God doing that—and he didn't. Instead, he chose to form people into *unique* representations of his glory. The multi-faceted nature of each person, combined with all the unique intricacies of other image-bearers, is meant to create a panoramic view of the glory of God.

The story of creation reveals that God built uniqueness into creation, including the first humans. We've already looked at the following passage that describes God's creation, but it's foundational for understanding all of God's story. So let's return to it:

> [24] *And God said, "Let the land produce living creatures according to their kinds: the livestock, the creatures that move along the ground, and the wild animals, each according to its kind." And it was so.* [25] *God made the wild animals according to their kinds, the livestock according to their kinds, and all the creatures that move along the ground according to their kinds. And God saw that it was good.*
>
> [26] *Then God said, "Let us make mankind in our image, in our likeness, so that they may rule over the fish in the sea and the birds in the sky, over the livestock and all the wild animals, and over all the creatures that move along the ground."*
>
> [27] *So God created mankind in his own image,*
> *in the image of God he created them;*
> *male and female he created them.*

> [28] *God blessed them and said to them, "Be fruitful and increase in number; fill the earth and subdue it. Rule over the fish in the sea and the birds in the sky and over every living creature that moves on the ground."*
>
> Genesis 1:24–28

All people are made in the image of God, but all people are not alike. God's design includes more than one person. He made two—male and female—and made each unique in some fundamental ways.

Men and women were both created by God and for God. They were both created in the image of God. There is no sense in stating that one gender is superior, or that one better reflects God's image than the other. Any sense of hierarchy in terms of the identity that men and women have is an aberration to God's plan. Both men and women are made for a relationship with God and to live on mission to reflect his glory to the world.

Still, men and women are different. Beyond the mere anatomical differences, there are many other ways the genders differ. Some of these differences reflect cultural trends and others may be attributable to sin's effect in a broken world, but that doesn't mean we should assume that gender differences don't matter. They do. There is a reason why God did not make all men or all women or make all humans gender neutral. He intended for men and women, uniquely, to reflect his image to the world in ways that would be impossible apart from this unique design.

These two genders were also designed to procreate so they would multiply and fill the earth (see Genesis 1:28). Again, God could have designed his world in any way he wanted, yet he chose sex between a married man and woman as the intended means of making more image-bearers. From the beginning, there was no aspect of human life that was outside the bounds of God's creative handiwork. Even sexuality was designed by God as a key part of his "very good" creation in the Garden of Eden.

There is no shortage of debate about these issues in our world. Gender is a subject of much contention. Children are often seen as a curse rather than a blessing.

Marriages fail at an alarming rate, and sexuality is perverted in innumerable ways. Still, we must be clear on one central truth—gender, sexuality, and childbearing are not the result of sin.

Before sin ever entered into God's story, gender, marriage, and sex already existed. It is true these areas of life were affected by human sin (see Genesis 3:14–19), as is every aspect of life in a broken world. There is no part of human existence that was not distorted when sin shattered the perfection of God's creation. Gender, sexuality, and marriage *are* affected by sin. But this doesn't mean we should abandon the intention behind God's good design.

Gender is a key aspect of his intricate design for image-bearers. Marriage is his plan for uniting one man and one woman in a lifelong, committed relationship. Sex is God's plan for intimacy in marriage and filling the earth with children who love him and others. They are all essential aspects of God's creation and aid his image-bearers in fulfilling his mission of filling the earth with his glory.

3. How does human culture showcase the glory of God? What can you learn about God from people who are vastly different from you?

4. What do you learn about God from the unique way in which he designed men and women?

God's Design for Marriage

The apostle Paul wrote the following to a church congregation in Ephesus:

> [22] *Wives, submit yourselves to your own husbands as you do to the Lord.* [23] *For the husband is the head of the wife as Christ is the head of the church, his body, of which he is the Savior.* [24] *Now as the church submits to Christ, so also wives should submit to their husbands in everything.*
>
> [25] *Husbands, love your wives, just as Christ loved the church and gave himself up for her* [26] *to make her holy, cleansing her by the washing with water through the word,* [27] *and to present her to himself as a radiant church, without stain or wrinkle or any other blemish, but holy and blameless.* [28] *In this same way, husbands ought to love their wives as their own bodies. He who loves his wife loves himself.* [29] *After all, no one ever hated their own body, but they feed and care for their body, just as Christ does the church—*[30] *for we are members of his body.* [31] *"For this reason a man will leave his father and mother and be united to his wife, and the two will become one flesh."* [32] *This is a profound mystery—but*

I am talking about Christ and the church. [33] *However, each one of you also must love his wife as he loves himself, and the wife must respect her husband."*

Ephesians 5:22-33

It's interesting to note that God is the one who saw a problem in the world he made. Even after declaring it very good, he saw that Adam was alone, so he created a helper fit for him (see Genesis 2:20). The word "helper" gives us a sense of the intention for gender and marriage. We need a helper when we have a mission or task that exceeds our capacity.

For instance, if you were moving a sofa out of a third-floor apartment, you might recruit a helper to carry the weight and maneuver a couch that is too large for you to handle alone. A college student might recruit a helper to tutor him or her in microeconomics or anatomy because the subject is too difficult. Helpers partner with someone else to accomplish a task.

The same is true in God's design. God provided Adam with Eve for more than just companionship. She was a gift designed to help him accomplish the mission of filling the earth with God's glory. The mission was so vast that Adam could not do it alone. Eve provided the perfect complement to Adam so that, together, they could fulfill the mission they were given by God.

Still today, God unites a man and woman in marriage for this purpose. Marriage is designed to help a man and woman fulfill God's mission. This is not to suggest that all people will be married, or that everyone should pursue marriage, but it is to say that if you do enter into marriage, the central purpose should be to partner together as helpers to fulfill God's purpose for your lives as a couple in a way neither of you could on your own.

If you are not married, the same premise still applies, as Paul notes:

[32] *I would like you to be free from concern. An unmarried man is concerned about the Lord's affairs—how he can please the Lord.* [33] *But a married man is concerned about the affairs of this world—how he can please his wife—*[34] *and his interests are divided. An unmarried woman or virgin is concerned about*

the Lord's affairs: Her aim is to be devoted to the Lord in both body and spirit. But a married woman is concerned about the affairs of this world—how she can please her husband. [35] *I am saying this for your own good, not to restrict you, but that you may live in a right way in undivided devotion to the Lord.*

1 Corinthians 7:32-35

Single men and women, according to Paul, can maintain an undivided focus on the mission of God. They will still need help along the way, so they can partner with other unique image-bearers in the church to invest their lives for eternal significance. Whether married or single, the focus of our lives is meant to be the greater mission God has given us. And all of our uniqueness—gender, personality, gifts, and passions—make it possible for us to work together to live out his mission in a myriad of unique ways.

5. Why is it important to remember that marriage, sex, childbearing, and gender are all God's design? What happens if we lose sight of his plan?

6. Why does Paul argue in 1 Corinthians 7:32–35 that it is better for some people to remain single? How can singleness aid in our mission to fill the earth with God's glory?

REFLECT

Uniqueness in Race, Ethnicities, and Cultures

Gender is not the only way in which humans are unique. In Acts 17:26, Paul points out that all people who have ever lived are descendants of the first man, Adam: "From one man he made all the nations, that they should inhabit the whole earth; and he marked out their appointed times in history and the boundaries of their lands." In the years since Adam, humans have spread out over the face of the earth and developed their own cultures and ethnicities.

The first human culture, in their pride, attempted to harness their power to make a name for themselves and build a tower to the heavens (see Genesis 9:1–9). They did not want to obey God's command to scatter and fill the earth. So God, in judgment, confused their languages and spread his people throughout the land.

The resulting races and cultures represent another manifestation of the creative brilliance of God. Physical appearance and language only scratch the surface of the ways that people differ from one another. Once again, this is all part of God's plan. Racism, and all other forms of bigotry, are an affront to God's purpose and plan for his creation. The diversity and uniqueness of humanity should be embraced and encouraged, not shunned or diminished.

7. What were the people attempting to do in the story told in Genesis 9:1–9?

8. Why should the uniqueness among humans be celebrated and encouraged instead of shunned or diminished?

Worthy of Respect

The differences in humanity can easily foster division and strife unless we remember there are far greater similarities uniting humanity than there are differences that divide. All people are made in the image of God and have a common origin in him. This means that everyone—regardless of age, gender, race, or socioeconomic standing—is worthy of dignity and respect. People should not have to earn value based on their performance. They should be deemed worthy simply because they are made in God's image to reflect his glory.

You are worthy of respect and love based simply on God's design and not your moral uprightness, your physical appearance, your work performance, or any feature you might use to define yourself. Comparison is the norm today in a world bustling with social media. It is easy to fall into the trap of sizing yourself up with others and asking, "Do I matter? Have I wasted my life? Why does my life look so average compared to everyone else's?"

The answer to these questions plaguing you—and the shame, guilt, and self-doubt that accompany them—doesn't come from trying to improve yourself in self-reliance to earn worthiness. You can spend your entire life playing that game, only to find that you harbor lingering doubts and insecurities. The only stable place to base your worth and value is in God.

9. What types of people are most difficult for you to love? What would change if you considered them in light of the fact that they were made in the image of God?

10. In what ways are you tempted to compare yourself to others? What are some of the consequences of falling into this trap?

CLOSE

The Psalmist described the intricate care that God took in creation: "For you created my inmost being; you knit me together in my mother's womb. I praise you because I am fearfully and wonderfully made; your works are wonderful, I know that full well" (Psalm 139:13–14).

The Creator of all made each person with his hands. He knit each one together long before the day he or she was born and declared that person to be wonderful. The One who said all of creation was "good" now claims that each person is "wonderful."

This verdict is the craving of every human soul. We long for someone to say that we are wonderful, and far too often, we make decisions based on how our actions might lead others to reach this conclusion. We post a picture in hopes that someone will validate us or invest frenzied work hours in the hopes that our performance will thrill our boss.

The conclusion we seek from others is one we've already been given by God. And, even better, God's verdict isn't dependent on our performance. His love is given simply because we are his—creatures made in his image.

The psalmist, reflecting on this reality, asks a profound question: "What is mankind that you are mindful of them, human beings that you care for them?" (Psalm 8:4). The psalmist is astounded by the love of God. He knows that people are frail and broken, twisted and distorted image-bearers. If God determined worth the way people do, nothing in men or women should cause God to love them. But God is not like us. He gives value and worth to everything he makes because of who he is. The uniqueness he builds into his world demonstrates the vast scope of his love. He can, and does, love all people—even you!

As you grow in understanding of your design and treasure your uniqueness, you are positioned to be used by God to fulfill his mission in the world. Think of all the time that's wasted in doubt, comparison, or fear because of an improper evaluation of yourself and others. What if you applied that time and mental energy to the purpose for which you were made? You might find that the story of your life started to make a bit more sense after all.

11. What have you learned about your unique design?

12. What are some ways that you see God using your unique design to make a difference in the world?

Lesson 5

WORK

"Fill the earth and subdue it. Rule over the fish in the sea and the birds in the sky and over every living creature that moves on the ground."

GENESIS 1:28

Whatever you do, work at it with all your heart, as working for the Lord.

COLOSSIANS 3:23

Whatever you do,
do it all
for the glory
of God.

— 1 CORINTHIANS 10:31

WELCOME

When I mention names like Billy Graham, Martin Luther King Jr., or Mother Teresa, most of us would recognize that they had a specific mission on the earth. God used their lives to impact others in meaningful ways. However, what some of us may not recognize is that the God of the universe has a specific mission for *all* of us. Our mission may not end up being written about in the history books, but it is unique and divinely inspired just the same.

We were made for a mission. God created work as a way to put on display the unique design he has for us and to bring glory to himself. Most of us will spend the majority of our lives working. That might sound like a depressing thought if the ideal life you imagine is one that consists of nothing but unending rest and leisure. For many, work is merely a necessary evil for obtaining the resources and time to truly enjoy life. Yes, work can be hard and toilsome.

The King of Queens, a popular television sitcom in the early 2000s, followed Doug Heffernan, played by Kevin James, who worked as a delivery man for a parcel delivery service. In one episode, he reflected on the nature of his work and mused that there was no grand purpose in delivering boxes. You, too, may feel that there is no purpose in what you do every day. But God had something else in mind when he created work. He intended your work to be fulfilling and soul satisfying.

Taking another look at the first chapter of Genesis informs us on how we should understand our careers and vocations. God tells Adam to be fruitful and multiply—a task he'll only be able to do with the help of his wife, Eve—and then says, "Be fruitful and increase in number; fill the earth and subdue it. Rule over the fish in the sea and the birds in the sky and over every living creature that moves on the ground" (Genesis 1:28).

Adam is given an amazing responsibility from God. He is to bring order to (subdue) and have dominion (rule) over every created thing God has made. From the beginning, God set up his world to function through the work of the men and women he created. He didn't create a mechanized universe arbitrarily controlled from the heavens. He chose to exercise his control of the world through the work of people.

Genesis 2 reveals a bit more about the nature of this work. God didn't simply place Adam in a garden and tell him to eat some good food, relax, and take a nap. Instead, God put him in the garden to "work it and take care of it" (Genesis 2:15). Work has been a part of God's story from the beginning. Like marriage, sexuality, gender, and children, work is not a result of human sin. We will see that work is more difficult because sin is in the picture—it will require toil and sweat to get the job done (see Genesis 3:18–19). But this doesn't mean work is evil.

You might be in a job that doesn't line up with how you are wired. You may think it is a meaningless dead end. If that describes you, there are a couple of aims for this lesson. The first is that you will be able to identify your unique wiring and put yourself on track to move toward that role as a vocation. The second is that that you would see opportunities, even if you are frustrated in your current job, to give God glory in it.

1. How does your current job line up with how you are uniquely wired?

2. What are some ways that God is being glorified through your current job?

READ

Stewards of Culture

Everything God does is for a purpose. There is not one activity in his world that is an accident or a result of luck. All of his creation was built with intentionality and specificity—including your role within it.

There is not one created thing that God himself did not have a hand in creating. He created the raw materials that form manmade things. But he didn't reveal the full potential of his created order all at once. That is where we come in. He created humanity to reveal, over time, the magnitude of his plan. For instance, he saw that cities would be part of his plan, and so he gifted human beings to envision, engineer, and build skyscrapers.

Everything that we do on this earth contributes to our culture. The question is, what kind of contribution are we making? Are we helping to create a culture that is self-glorifying or one that puts the spotlight in its rightful place? Craig Bartholomew and Barry Goheen wrote the following about God's purpose in creating humanity:

> *God's call to us to "have dominion" over his creation entails this sort of compliment to what we are capable of achieving as his stewards. It also brings a correspondingly heavy responsibility for what comes out of our stewardship. If this is what being "in the image of God" involves, then clearly our service for God is to be as wide as the creation itself and will include taking good care of the environment.*[1]

The following passages in Genesis lay the groundwork of what God envisioned for humanity's role in his creation:

> *God blessed them and said to them, "Be fruitful and increase in number; fill the earth and subdue it. Rule over the fish in the sea and the birds in the sky and over every living creature that moves on the ground."*
>
> Genesis 1:28

> [4] *This is the account of the heavens and the earth when they were created, when the LORD God made the earth and the heavens.* [5] *Now no shrub had yet appeared on the earth and no plant had yet sprung up, for the LORD God had not sent rain on the earth and there was no one to work the ground,* [6] *but streams came up from the earth and watered the whole surface of the ground.* [7] *Then the LORD God formed a man from the dust of the ground and breathed into his nostrils the breath of life, and the man became a living being.*
>
> Genesis 2:4–7

> [15] *The LORD God took the man and put him in the Garden of Eden to work it and take care of it.* [16] *And the LORD God commanded the man, "You are free to eat from any tree in the garden;* [17] *but you must not eat from the tree of the knowledge of good and evil, for when you eat from it you will certainly die."*
>
> Genesis 2:15–17

3. According to these passages in Genesis, what existed on the earth prior to someone working it?

4. Take some time to reflect on the aspects of creation that you benefit from every day (house, car, paper, computer, etc.). Think about the progression from raw material to what you enjoy today. How many different inventions and inventors where necessary?

Finding Our Roles

Orville and Wilbur Wright are often credited for inventing the airplane. This honor is rightly placed on them and a handful of other aviation pioneers. However, long before their historic flight in Kitty Hawk, North Carolina, the foundation for modern aviation had already been established.

The Wright Brothers ran a bicycle shop in their hometown of Dayton, Ohio. It was in this shop that they tinkered on modifications to the bicycle, even coming up with some of their own original designs. Little did they know that the early days of their work would ultimately lead to inventing modern aviation as we know it today. Over time, as they worked in their shop, their vision for the airplane came to fruition.

Amazingly, several years prior to the first flight, a newspaper editor saw the correlation between the bicycle and the airplane. He said in 1896, "The flying machine problem is liable to be solved by bicycle inventors. The flying machine will not be in the same shape, or at all in the style of the numerous kinds of cycles, but the study to produce a light, swift machine is likely to lead to an evolution in which wings will play a conspicuous part."[2]

In 1418, an Italian engineer named Giovanni Fontana constructed a human-powered device consisting of four wheels and a loop of rope connected by gears. Around the same time, Leonardo da Vinci was credited with inventing the "chain and the cog." Another 450 years later, more inventors improved on the design of the pedals.

Dozens, if not hundreds, of people have had their hand in the perfection of the bicycle over many centuries. Many of them were not thinking that somehow their little invention would make it possible for humans to fly. They were just playing the role they were designed to play at the time God had ordained for them to play it.

We all have a role to play, and that role is a part of a bigger story. We have no idea how our work today may impact the future, but everything we do is a part of God's bigger, mostly unseen plan. Parents don't know the impact their kids and grandkids will have. Plumbers don't know who might live in one of their houses and the impact those homeowners will have on the world. Writers don't know who is reading their work and what it will accomplish.

Scripture tells us that "whatever" we do, we should do for the glory of God. You may be struggling with your calling. You may feel that what you are doing is insignificant. You may be wondering, "Where do I start?" The best place to start is with what is in front of you—to get up every day and say, "Whatever I do today, I am going to do it for God and his glory."

> [23] *Whatever you do, work at it with all your heart, as working for the Lord, not for human masters,* [24] *since you know that you will receive an inheritance from the Lord as a reward. It is the Lord Christ you are serving.*
>
> Colossians 3:23–24

5. How should this Scripture change your perspective on your current work situation?

6. Can you see how your role, even if it seems insignificant, is a part of God's larger plan? Explain.

REFLECT

Scattered into the World

We began this lesson with the statement, "you were made for a mission." Hopefully, you have been able to see the clear connection between God's mission and your work. The overall mission of God is to fill the earth with his glory. He wants everyone, everywhere, to know how great he is. His plan to accomplish this mission is to create unique image-bearers who can scatter into all the world and represent him.

This scattering can, and does, happen geographically. God's people live in Bangladesh, Istanbul, New York, Santo Domingo . . . all around the earth . . . and it happens as God's people scatter into their vocations in these cities. It's easy to believe that those who really love God, who give of themselves to his mission, must become pastors or missionaries. Not necessarily! Some become lawyers, teachers, plumbers, or politicians. Mission, rightly understood, involves anything God's people do to bring order, exercise leadership, or foster creativity in the places they live in such a way that God's glory is seen and people worship him.

Since God's Spirit lives inside every Christian, God goes with them into these vocations, empowering them to reflect his glory there (see Romans 8:9; 1 Corinthians

3:16). So, while you might think you are wasting your life at your job, remember that you can be in this job on a mission for however long you might work there. If you know Jesus, God has positioned your life to declare and demonstrate his glory through whatever work you put your hands to doing. If you do not consider yourself a Christian, it may be that God has positioned your life around other believers to hear and see the gospel at work in them. Work done to the glory of God is a crucial way God's mission advances in our world (see 1 Corinthians 10:31).

Again, one of the great fallacies that has crept into the church in recent years is the idea that only professional pastors and missionaries can serve God in a meaningful way. This line of thinking has sidelined many into believing their profession is somehow less of an important calling. There is no doubt that pastors and missionaries are a part of God's story, but so are film producers, teachers, moms, accountants, and janitors. You have been given access to a group of people that your pastor, most likely, will not have consistent access to. God has placed you there as his ambassador.

7. Who are some of the people that God has given you access to that your pastor or others in the church do not? How are you taking advantage of that opportunity?

8. How might God be using you to be a consistent witness in the lives of your family, friends, coworkers, and others in your community?

The Value of Work . . . and Rest

Many assume God is going to obliterate his world in the end—that because sin has broken his good creation, he is simply going to come back, get his people, take them to heaven, and annihilate the world once they're gone. But this is not at all the picture the Bible paints. Rather, Scripture describes God purifying the world that he has made (see 2 Peter 3:7). That's what fire does. It takes off the impurities and exposes what is pure.

God's plan does not end with him destroying this world. Instead, he is going to make it new. John's vision of the end of the world in the book of Revelation shows God coming down from heaven and once again making his dwelling with his holy people in a purified world (see Revelation 21:1–4). This new world will be free from sin and its implications forever.

This means the work we do in this life to display God's creativity, power, and perfection is not temporary. We are partnering with God in the work he is doing to make all things new. As we invest our lives in meaningful work, we are getting a jump-start on eternity.

In fact, since God established meaningful work before sin entered his world, we can assume there will still be meaningful work for us to do in heaven. We won't simply sit around on clouds and play harps all day. Instead, we will give our lives to work that showcases the glory of God. In heaven, we will have the joy of doing this work in a world that is free from sin. No longer will the curse reign, so our new bodies, which are free from sin, will allow our work to cultivate and care for a world that is free from sin too.

One final point needs to be made about work—another truth built into God's original design. Once God finished creating all things, including people to reflect his image, he spent the seventh day resting. We would expect this from a human. After a demanding eight-hour workday, most of us crash on the couch in exhaustion. Work drains our energy and strength, and we need to recover. But God is infinitely powerful. He doesn't grow tired or weary—not even after spending six days making everything in the universe.

So, why did he rest? We discover his plan for rest in this passage:

> [8] *"Remember the Sabbath day by keeping it holy.* [9] *Six days you shall labor and do all your work,* [10] *but the seventh day is a sabbath to the Lord your God. On it you shall not do any work, neither you, nor your son or daughter, nor your male or female servant, nor your animals, nor any foreigner residing in your towns.* [11] *For in six days the Lord made the heavens and the earth, the sea, and all that is in them, but he rested on the seventh day. Therefore the Lord blessed the Sabbath day and made it holy.*
>
> Exodus 20:8–11

God's rest sets a pattern for people to follow. This six-and-one, work-and-rest rhythm was to be the norm among God's people in the Old Testament. The day of rest was holy—set apart for worshiping God. When we say the day was designed for worship, we mean more than simply gathering with other people, hearing from God, singing songs, and praying prayers. This is important, but the entire day was meant to demonstrate the worth of God.

By doing no work, the people were declaring that God was worth more than whatever goods or resources they might have earned through an extra day of labor. They were also declaring their trust in God to provide for their needs—even if they took a day off and did no work. This dependence and trust would clearly distinguish God's people from the other nations who never stopped working out of reliance on human abilities and efforts alone.

Although Christians are not bound by the Old Testament law, we should continue to trust God enough to rest from our work. Rest means more than a lazy day around the house. It means intentionally creating rhythms in life that remind us that neither work nor the accumulation of worldly resources is the chief end of life.

We must reject the temptation to constantly fret about our lives and instead relentlessly trust God to meet our needs (see Matthew 6:25–34). Rest reminds us that God is capable of accomplishing his mission and taking care of our lives without us. He doesn't need us, but in his grace, he chooses to use us as we invest in meaningful work that brings him glory.

9. What would change about your work if you really believed that what you were doing now could count for all eternity?

10. What are some of the challenges you face when it comes to taking a "Sabbath" day of rest for the Lord each week?

CLOSE

God created work in the beginning, and like all things he made, he designed it to fill the earth with his glory. You don't have to relegate God to the periphery of your life and the aspects of it that you think are "spiritual," like going to church or reading your Bible. God isn't just concerned about these aspects of your life. He also cares about all the hours you will invest in work throughout your life. Done intentionally with faithfulness, humility, and excellence, work becomes another aspect of your story that fits into the grand story God has been writing throughout human history.

So never downplay the importance of the role that God has given you to play. You may be in a season of transition, moving from one job to the next. You might even be in a season of wrestling, trying to discern God's plan. Regardless, you can rest in the fact that God's ultimate purpose in your vocation is to glorify him.

11. In what ways would the world be missing out if you did not use your gifts?

12. Are there any changes that you need to make to better align your gifts and your vocation?

Notes

1. Craig Bartholomew and Barry Goheen, *The Drama of Scripture: Finding Our Place in the Biblical Story* (Baker Academic, 2004), pp. 37–38.
2. Quoted in Margaret Guroff, "The Untold Story of How Bicycle Design Led to the Invention of the Airplane," Fast Company, https://www.fastcompany.com/3061592/the-untold-story-of-how-bicycle-design-led-to-the-invention-of-the-airplane.

Lesson 6

COMMUNITY

"It is not good for the man to be alone. I will make a helper suitable for him."

GENESIS 2:18

All the believers were together and had everything in common.

ACTS 2:44

And let us . . .
spur one another
on toward love
and good deeds.

— HEBREWS 10:24

WELCOME

Life is hard! But it is even harder when you try to do it alone. People were meant to live in relationship to one another. Regardless of how independent or self-sufficient you are, the reality is that you need other people in your life.

The Bible refers to this need for each other as being like "iron sharpens iron" (Proverbs 27:17), or like a body of parts working together to accomplish a collective good (see 1 Corinthians 12:12–31). Scripture also says it is just not good for us to be alone (see Genesis 2:18).

An incredible couple, Dave and Kathy, are anchors in our church. Most weeks, you will find them on the front row, leading others in worship by their example. Several years ago, tragedy struck when their daughter "Tini" was killed in an automobile accident along with three of her college friends. In the subsequent years, I have watched our local church rally around them, determined they wouldn't have to walk through this unimaginable circumstance alone.

I couldn't fathom life without people around me. First and foremost, my family are my immediate community. My wife is my partner in ministry and life, and we spur each other on to become all that God intended for us.

Second, my church family has my back. I know they will be there through the mountain tops and valleys of life. Finally, my neighbors (many of whom are a part of our church) are a constant source of encouragement and a joy to do life with.

1. List a few occasions when the people around you have been there for you:

A. A time of encouragement:

B. A time of sorrow:

C. A time of accountability:

D. A time of teaching:

E. A time of celebration:

2. In the space provided, reflect on your gratitude for having your community around you during these occasions.

READ

Made for Relationships

We were made for friendship and companionship. All our lives are a reflection of the community around us. Family and friends shape every aspect of our being. The imprint of our parents, teachers, pastors, friends, children, grandchildren, coworkers, and spouses can be found in all of us. God, in his grace, has recognized this from the beginning. In the very opening pages of Scripture, the truth that humans were not supposed to do life alone is front and center, as we read in the following passage from Genesis:

> [18] *The Lord God said, "It is not good for the man to be alone. I will make a helper suitable for him."*
>
> [19] *Now the Lord God had formed out of the ground all the wild animals and all the birds in the sky. He brought them to the man to see what he would name them; and whatever the man called each living creature, that was its name.* [20] *So the man gave names to all the livestock, the birds in the sky and all the wild animals.*
>
> *But for Adam no suitable helper was found.* [21] *So the Lord God caused the man to fall into a deep sleep; and while he was sleeping, he took one of the man's ribs and*

then closed up the place with flesh. [22] *Then the* L*ORD* *God made a woman from the rib he had taken out of the man, and he brought her to the man.*

[23] *The man said,*

"This is now bone of my bones
and flesh of my flesh;
she shall be called 'woman,'
for she was taken out of man."

[24] *That is why a man leaves his father and mother and is united to his wife, and they become one flesh.*

[25] *Adam and his wife were both naked, and they felt no shame."*

Genesis 2:18–25

Adam was given Eve to help him accomplish his mission in the world. But there's more than merely a functional relationship at play in this chapter of Genesis. God sees there is a problem with the good world he made—that something is not right. Adam is alone.

Adam is not the one to point this out to God. We don't read about him walking through the garden begging God for a wife. Rather, God sees it is not good for Adam to be alone, so he gives Adam a gift to address this void. The woman is literally bone of Adam's bones and flesh of his flesh, which is a picture of the relational oneness that God intended for the first couple.

They are one-flesh—an intentional model of intimate relationship between the Father, Son, and Holy Spirit. From that time forward, God intended for a husband and wife to leave their families of origin and be united to one another in permanent oneness. Paul, writing to the church in Ephesus, points to marriage as a picture of the way God loves His church. Everything about the marriage relationship is meant to show the world the love of God:

[22] Wives, submit yourselves to your own husbands as you do to the Lord. [23] For the husband is the head of the wife as Christ is the head of the church, his body, of which he is the Savior. [24] Now as the church submits to Christ, so also wives should submit to their husbands in everything.

[25] Husbands, love your wives, just as Christ loved the church and gave himself up for her [26] to make her holy, cleansing her by the washing with water through the word, [27] and to present her to himself as a radiant church, without stain or wrinkle or any other blemish, but holy and blameless. [28] In this same way, husbands ought to love their wives as their own bodies. He who loves his wife loves himself. [29] After all, no one ever hated their own body, but they feed and care for their body, just as Christ does the church— [30] for we are members of his body. [31] "For this reason a man will leave his father and mother and be united to his wife, and the two will become one flesh." [32] This is a profound mystery—but I am talking about Christ and the church. [33] However, each one of you also must love his wife as he loves himself, and the wife must respect her husband.

Ephesians 5:22-33

3. If you are married, how can your marriage accomplish this goal of revealing the love of God to the world?

4. If you are not currently married but expect to one day be, what would change about your pursuit of marriage by understanding that the most fundamental goal is to paint a picture of God's love?

Sin's Effect and God's Solution

Relational harmony between the first husband and wife was meant to have a spillover effect into their other relationships. Through fruitful multiplication, God's people would make more and more image-bearers with whom they could live together in unity and love. But sin wreaked havoc on this goal. Now, human relationships would be grueling. Adam and Eve would no longer work together in perfect unity and mission. They would strive to control and rule over one another (see Genesis 3:16). They would be more prone to division and disunity—as demonstrated by the first murder (see Genesis 4)—than love and unity.

Yet God did not abandon his goal for human relationships, even though sin had distorted and broken his design. He continues to call his people to love one another as a reflection of his love for each person in the Trinity. The nation of Israel, whose story is told through the Old Testament, is intended to model the love that God intended from creation.

When reading the Ten Commandments, many point out that you can boil them down to two central requirements: love God and love others. Jesus, when asked what was the most important, or greatest, of all the Law, said exactly that: "'Love the Lord your God with all your heart and with all your soul and with all your mind and with all your strength . . . 'Love your neighbor as yourself.' There is no commandment greater than these" (Mark 12:30–31).

Jesus summarized the entire law in a word—*love*. This love works outward in two directions: first, vertically toward God; and second, horizontally toward others made in God's image. Jesus makes it clear in the story of the Good Samaritan that this love should know no bounds (see Luke 10:25–37). We are called to do more than love those who are like us and can reciprocate our love. Since all people are made in God's image, every person you meet is worthy of love.

The Old Testament can be summed up as the people of God being overwhelming failures at loving God and loving one another. The implications of human sin are insurmountable. Division becomes the norm, leading to a civil war within Israel and the demise of God's people. Even so, once again, God does not give up.

Our entire study of *Beginnings* has shown us that every aspect of God's creation has a plan and purpose. None of it is accidental or haphazard. Humanity's relationship to work, the earth, and each other all has a specific purpose.

As we journey into the New Testament, we see this special design for community played out in a new area—the church. God sends his Son, Jesus, to model the love he intends (see Romans 5:8). Much can be said about the love of Jesus, but we can focus on its fulfillment of these two great commands: he was perfect in his love of God and perfect in his love of others. As we will see in a future study from this series, God designed the Church to be the hands and feet of Jesus on earth to fulfill Jesus' prayer that the kingdom of God would come "on earth as it is in heaven" (Matthew 6:10).

In John's Gospel, Jesus makes a statement so astounding, so controversial, that it ultimately gets him killed. He says that he and his Father are one (see John 10:30). Jesus is able to forgive sins and heal the sick because he is God and because he operates in perfect relational harmony with the other members of the Trinity. Later, he rebukes Philip for asking him to show him God, the Father. Jesus says, "Anyone who has seen me has seen the Father. . . . Don't you believe that I am in the Father, and that the Father is in me?" (John 14:9–10).

There is no division within God. He is One, even as he exists in three persons. The relational intimacy that God designed men and women to have with him is modeled perfectly in the relationship between the Father, the Son, and the Holy Spirit. Jesus was also perfect in his love for people. His care for the marginalized and outcasts was so great that many mocked him, accusing him of being a glutton and a drunkard because he spent so much time around the riff-raff of humanity (see Matthew 11:18–19). He tenderly cared for the sick and taught the wayward—even those society had long since abandoned (see John 4).

The extent of this love is seen most vividly in his sacrificial death on a Roman cross (see Philippians 2:4–11). There, Jesus willingly took on the form of a servant and gave his life to pay the price for human sin. His love wasn't mere emotion—it was active. He made intentional decisions to love, even when he knew those actions would result in his brutal death.

Those who have been transformed by God's power—those filled by his Spirit and sent into the world to reflect his image—will model this love in their human relationships. The defining mark of God's people is love (see Matthew 22:26–30; John 13:35). The church, like the nation of Israel, is called to demonstrate this type of love. Luke gives an example of life in the early church in this account found in the book of Acts:

> [42] *They devoted themselves to the apostles' teaching and to fellowship, to the breaking of bread and to prayer.* [43] *Everyone was filled with awe at the many wonders and signs performed by the apostles.* [44] *All the believers were together and had everything in common.* [45] *They sold property and possessions to give to anyone who had need.* [46] *Every day they continued to meet together in the temple courts. They broke bread in their homes and ate together with glad and sincere hearts,* [47] *praising God and enjoying the favor of all the people. And the Lord added to their number daily those who were being saved.*
>
> Acts 2:42–47

These church communities were especially amazing in the way they united unique people. The fundamental human conflict in the Old Testament was between Jews and Gentiles. As Paul wrote, the Gentiles were "excluded from citizenship in Israel and foreigners to the covenants of the promise" (Ephesians 2:12). As a result of sin, a dividing wall existed between people, separating them from one another. However, Jesus came and "destroyed the barrier" (Ephesians 2:14). Now, in the church, there is "neither Jew nor Gentile, neither slave nor free, nor is there male and female, for you are all one in Christ Jesus" (Galatians 3:28).

Jesus makes it possible for all of these diverse types of people to know the love of God and experience love with one another in the community of the Church.

5. How does sin hurt all human relationships? How has sin affected your own relationships?

6. How is the cross a picture of the way we are called to love other people?

REFLECT

Agents of Restoration

If we are not careful, we can read about God's design for community with an unrealistic, utopian lens. We can assume from the descriptions of communities of God's people in the Old and New Testaments that they were perfect.

In reality, all of our attempts at community building are messy and imperfect. There are no perfect churches, just like there are no perfect marriages, workplaces, or neighborhoods. The impact of the Fall on all of humanity is evidenced all around us. This is why, as indicated in the opening sentence of this lesson, life is hard.

Because of sin, our human attempts at building relationships will always lead to dead ends. The good news, however, is that we can live our lives through Jesus' power. Our ability to be in community is not dependent on our own strength but rather is made possible because of Jesus' work on the cross. Scripture says that through Christ we are being reconciled to each other (see 2 Corinthians 5:18). He gives us the ministry of reconciliation to act as agents of restoration in our community.

7. How have you learned to rely on God's wisdom and ability more than your own understanding when you experience conflicts with others?

8. How has God used you as a minister of reconciliation in your relationships?

The Mindset of Christ

Without grace, building and maintaining relationships would be impossible—and grace *is* impossible without Jesus. Paul instructed the church in Philippi, "Do nothing out of selfish ambition or vain conceit. Rather, in humility value others above yourselves, not looking to your own interests but each of you to the interests of the others" (Philippians 2:3–4).

This all sounds well and good, but the question still remains: how do we look to the interests of others over our own interests? The answer comes in the next verse: "In your relationships with one another, have the same mindset as Christ Jesus" (verse 5).

We see that "having the mindset of Jesus" means being willing to lay down our lives for others. When we take up this self-sacrificial mindset ourselves, seeking others' interests above our own won't seem so out of the norm. Helping our spouse with the dishes will seem like a pretty small sacrifice. Dropping what we're doing to meet a friend with a flat tire will be a given. Making a financial sacrifice to help meet our church's needs will be par for the course.

9. How could changing your mindset about your relationships change the way that you approach the people in them?

10. Take a few moments to name some of the ways that Jesus sacrificed for others:

A. In the desert for forty days (see Matthew 4:1–11):

B. In the Garden of Gethsemane (see Matthew 26:36–36):

C. On the cross (see Luke 23:26-43):

D. Other ways that come to mind:

CLOSE

Our chaotic lives often obscure God's story. We grow consumed with the unique twists-and-turns that our lives bring. Much like a kid on a carnival ride, we can become dizzy with the pace of life and lose focus on why we exist in the first place. The resulting disorientation often leads to a life of random busyness that lacks purpose or direction. At times, we might sedate the pain in our lives through sin. Other times, we simply learn to live with a nagging sense that something is not right.

God has a better plan. He is intent on calling us into a bigger story—one that spans from the creation of the world into eternity. We don't have to wander through life without direction. Instead, we can throw ourselves into God's grand mission. In this story—and in this story alone—we can find our lives actually beginning to make sense for the first time.

Fighting for healthy relationships with others is not as easy as it seems, and it is impossible without Jesus. We need to continually look to him for our example as we seek to live our lives in community.

11. What are some practical ways that you need the people around you to live your calling?

12. If you do not have a healthy community around you, what are some practical steps you can take to move in that direction?

NEXT

God is the author of the story of creation. His story is one that includes every intricate detail, including you. In these six lessons in *Beginnings*, we have seen that God is all powerful and majestic yet still knows everything about us. In fact, we were written into his story from the very beginning to lead lives of purpose.

In *Revolt,* the next study in this series, we will see how sin entered into the world and explore its effects on humanity. We will see the impact of this rebellion and how it muddies up the plan and purpose God has for us. Ultimately, we will see how God redeems and restores us, but first we must confront the realities of a broken world.

Thank you for stepping into this journey! Stay the course. God has a lot that he wants to do in your life!

LEADER'S GUIDE

Thank you for your willingness to lead your group through this study. What you have chosen to do is valuable and will make a great difference in the lives of others. The rewards of being a leader are different from those of participating, and we hope that as you lead you will find your own walk with Jesus deepened by the experience.

The lessons in this study guide are suitable for church classes, Bible studies, and small groups. Each lesson is structured to provoke thought and help you grow in your knowledge and understanding of Christ. There are multiple components in this section that can help you structure your lessons and discussion time, so make sure you read and consider each one.

BEFORE YOU BEGIN

Before your first meeting, make sure the group members have a copy of this study guide so they can follow along and have their answers written out ahead of time. Alternately, you can hand out the study guides at your first meeting and give the group members some time to look over the material and ask any preliminary questions. During your first meeting, be sure to send a sheet of paper around the room and have the members write down their name, phone number, and email address so you can keep in touch with them during the week.

Generally, the ideal size for a group is eight to ten people, which will ensure that everyone has enough time to participate in discussions. If you have more people, you might want to break up the main group into smaller subgroups. Encourage those who show up at the first meeting to commit to attending the duration of the study. This will help the group members get to know one another, create stability for the group, and help you, as the leader, know how to best prepare each week.

Try to initiate a free-flowing discussion as you go through each lesson. Invite group members to bring any questions they have or insights they discover as they go through the content to the next meeting, especially if they were unsure of the meaning of some parts of the lesson. Be prepared to discuss the biblical truth that relates to each topic in the study.

WEEKLY PREPARATION

As the group leader, here are a few things you can do to prepare for each meeting:

- Make sure you understand the content of the lesson so you know how to structure group time and are prepared to lead group discussion.
- Depending on how much time you have each week, you may not be able to reflect on every question. Select specific questions that you feel will evoke the best discussion.
- At the end of your discussion, take prayer requests from your group members and pray for each other.

STRUCTURING THE DISCUSSION TIME

It is up to you to keep track of the time and keep things on schedule. You might want to set a timer for each question that you discuss so both you and the group members know when your time is up. (There are some good phone apps for timers that play a gentle chime or other pleasant sound instead of a disruptive noise.)

Don't be concerned if the group members are quiet or slow to share. People are often quiet when they are pulling together their ideas, and this might be a new experience for them. Just ask a question and let it hang in the air until someone shares. You can then say, "Thank you. What about others? What thoughts came to you?"

If you need help in organizing your time when planning your group Bible study, the following schedule, for sixty minutes and ninety minutes, can give you a structure for the lesson:

	60 Minutes	90 Minutes
Welcome: Arrive and get settled	5 minutes	10 minutes
Message: Review the lesson	15 minutes	25 minutes
Discussion: Discuss study questions	35 minutes	45 minutes
Prayer: Pray together and dismiss	5 minutes	10 minutes

GROUP DYNAMICS

Leading a group through *Beginnings* will prove to be highly rewarding both to you and your group members. But you still may encounter challenges along the way! Discussions can get off track. Group members may not be sensitive to the needs and ideas of others. Some might worry they will be expected to talk about matters that make them feel awkward. Others may express comments that result in disagreements. To help ease this strain on you and the group, consider the following ground rules:

- When someone raises a question or comment that is off the main topic, suggest you deal with it another time, or, if you feel led to go in that direction, let the group know you will be spending some time discussing it.
- If someone asks a question that you don't know how to answer, admit it and move on. At your discretion, feel free to invite group members to comment on questions that call for personal experience.
- If you find one or two people are dominating the discussion time, direct a few questions to others in the group. Outside the main group time, ask the

more dominating members to help you draw out the quieter ones. Work to make them a part of the solution instead of the problem.

- When a disagreement occurs, encourage the group members to process the matter in love. Encourage those on opposite sides to restate what they heard the other side say about the matter, and then invite each side to evaluate if that perception is accurate. Lead the group in examining other Scriptures related to the topic and look for common ground.

When any of these issues arise, encourage your group members to follow these words from the Bible: "Love one another" (John 13:34), "If it is possible, as far as it depends on you, live at peace with everyone" (Romans 12:18), "Whatever is true . . . noble . . . right . . . if anything is excellent or praiseworthy—think about such things" (Philippians 4:8), and "Be quick to listen, slow to speak and slow to become angry" (James 1:19). This will make your group time more rewarding and beneficial for everyone who attends.

Thank you again for your willingness to lead your group. May God reward your efforts and dedication, equip you to guide your group in the weeks ahead, and make your time together fruitful for his kingdom.

ABOUT THE AUTHORS

Aaron Coe has spent more than twenty years working in the non-profit and philanthropic space. Much of that time was spent in New York City in the years after 9/11, helping with revitalization efforts. Aaron served as vice president at North American Mission Board, providing strategic guidance and leadership. He has also worked with organizations like Passion, illumiNations, Food for the Hungry, the Ethics and Religious Liberty Commission, and many others. Aaron has a Ph.D. in Applied Theology and teaches at Dallas Theological Seminary. He is the founder of Future City Now, which seeks to help visionary leaders maximize their influence in the world. Additionally, Aaron served as the General Editor of *The Jesus Bible*. Aaron lives in Atlanta with his wife, Carmen, and their four children.

Matt Rogers holds a Ph.D. in Applied Theology and teaches and writes on Christian mission, ministry, and discipleship. Notably, Matt served as the lead writer for the best-selling *The Jesus Bible*. He and his wife, Sarah, and their five children live in Greenville, South Carolina, where Matt serves as the pastor of Christ Fellowship Cherrydale.

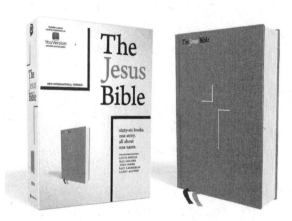

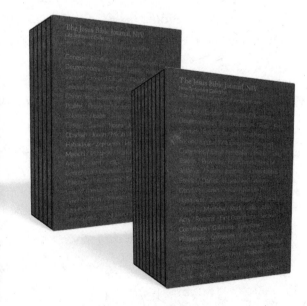

Video Study for Your Church or Small Group

In this six-session video Bible study, bestselling author and pastor Louie Giglio helps you apply the principles in *Don't Give the Enemy a Seat at Your Table* to your life. The study guides includes access to six streaming video sessions, video notes and a comprehensive structure for group discussion time, and personal study for deeper reflection between sessions.

Study Guide + Streaming Video
9780310156284

DVD
9780310134268

Available now at your favorite bookstore
or streaming video on StudyGateway.com.

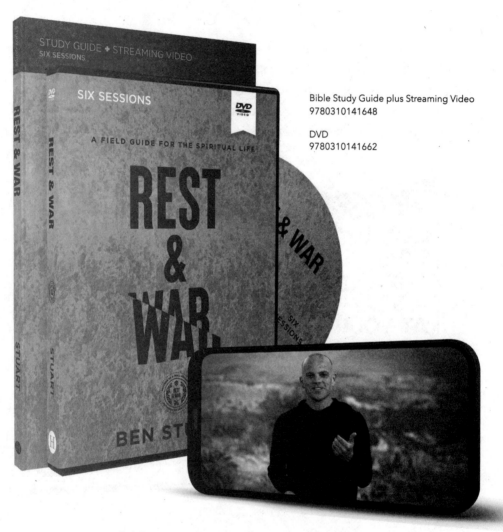